The Star in the Branches

James Peake has worked in trade publishing for several years. He lives in London with his wife and son.

Also by Two Rivers Poets

The Star in the Branches

James Peake

TWO
RIVERS
PRESS

First published in the UK in 2022 by Two Rivers Press
7 Denmark Road, Reading RG1 5PA.
www.tworiverspress.com

ISBN 978-1-909747-95-1

1 2 3 4 5 6 7 8 9

Two Rivers Press is represented in the UK by Inpress Ltd
and distributed by Ingram Publisher Services UK.

Cover design and illustration by Sally Castle
Text design by Nadja Guggi and typeset in Janson and Parisine

Printed and bound in Great Britain by Severn, Gloucester

Acknowledgements

My thanks are due to the editors of the following where certain of these
poems first appeared: *Wild Court*, *NU Review*, *Raceme* and *The Spectator*.

Contents

Electronic noise
is knowledge
and the street light
loves us

In memory of William Lyon Bowie

I.

The Angel of Unsustainable Complexity

I.

They brought you to brightness with MRI,
made legible the sealed interior,
rainbowing storms of pure thought and feeling,
a language of colour like medieval glass.

The neurologist is rightly proud of what he shows,
points out detail with a bitten pencil.

In Mann's *The Magic Mountain*, one cousin asks another
for permission before looking at his X-ray
like you or I might knock at a bathroom door.

And other side-on thoughts occur,
of the ice inside your girlhood windows
and fondly recalled by you for decades

because of the frugal life they implied
and because they meant you'd woken
in the house of your father, and he is alive.

2.

Things worth knowing in a time and place
of my choosing would include silence,
its cultivation, its response to love.
Much worth knowing doesn't travel,
textbooks fall out of date,
Anaximenes blows into his hands
because air, like language under pressure,
changes temperature, then illustrated tales
of the Galilean, kindly and Caucasian.
Crackle of rainfall, an overwhelmed London,
acres of floodwater, the Royal parks and monuments,
the drowned volutes of car parks.
In the Georgian reptile house a lizard
sets foot between the atoms of a pane of glass.

3.

The children are learning our ways
at home, in the street, online,
listening and watching while awake
and at other times you wouldn't credit.
Number, colour, shape and value,
what we conceal or attempt to,
what is shown deliberately or by accident,
how the visible parts forget
that others watch like we watch them.
An object which knows itself
from inside. But knows what?
What mirrors broadcast, a flash
of canine or a dilated pupil,
each accident of appearance given back,
belonging instantly to the past.

4.

A face asleep is trustworthy and stupid,
intersubjective object, fallen back
to base structure, eyes closed to the light,
mouth open. The inner person
and the outer have swapped ends of the lead.
I drool sometimes, whatever that might mean.

I woke early and think of our close friends
just broken up, or just able to let close friends know.
I hear the first train as a rhythm
in the sofa arm under my head. Work soon.

That journey from stranger to lover and back
is not exact, a return to an unchanged place,
more like a face lit up by wakefulness
until the next and clockwork closure,
almost the same, new things to remember.

5.

I had in the single earphone from Dad's
superseded radio, like a bar of lead
on my turned-down blanket and chest,
the tuning broad and slightly adrift.
Voices surged into it like weather,
broken or scuffed on the north-west edge
of what had been my granddad's cottage.

A parent myself before I guessed
what Dad's gentle drollery contained,
as much delight in timing and wit,
of releasing laughter in his children,
as refusal to hand down rage
without origin, witnessed
when young and stayed host to,
the cost to himself, the catcher, my father.

6.

Who said we're not evil enough? Or
that what we love tells us what we are?
Eyes put out, throats cut, for coltan
so I can play games on the Central Line.
The guy who mended this screen
said no two breakages are the same
and hairlines in glass can be divined.
Metaphors feign continuity
between known and novel,
think carbon copy, mining, window,
the once and future rank of words.
Eight hours of commute, more,
a day a week almost unaccounted for,
during which I've touched nothing changeable,
have added nothing to the available real.

7.

What you really loved from afar,
more perhaps than other, sanctioned things,
will be shown, laid out as a lifetime
of data, audited decades of search,
harvest of your innermost, and you
not fluid, thoughtful, original
in the ways you'd once assumed,
the appetite, preoccupation,
stored in perpetuity, unfulfilled.
The unholy mess of my digitised self,
a wake of fragments representing me
in which someone else controls the rights.
Mr P was this you? When me-not-me
has been more places than I can
remember, care or would admit to.

8.

A foreign city is sameness, strangeness,
process and novelty, can we at least agree
on the time zone, that I shouldn't call home
even if I wanted to? Images of friends
aren't company but revenue (we know)
and since I landed every other yawn
tastes of bubble bath. For no reason,
something briefly off in the brain. Don't
inflict boredom, it's your own problem.
My mother and hers behind her would say so.
Key features are internalised -
driveway, junction, edge - the rest
then implied, like we know a hotel
has other rooms, and within those rooms
other guests, more or less alive.

9.

Convergent discoveries give texture
to experience, are grist to compare.
Take shadows, solidified
unfrozen to an incoherent mind,
the fallacy then of imitative form
applied to dementia, gaps in the text,
glitch, non-sequitur, the elapsed
awareness of a fridge when it stops.
Oh. A ragged edge of fresh concrete,
soon a club in which moneyed tourists
are reborn, the floor under them swollen
like text on a balloon, they'll move
from that surface not as their brain
or job description, but as swimmers
in the primaries flooding the room.

10.

Vanished flowers reappear in the grass,
thyme, speedwell, in the guise of themselves
because there is no excess, all things
relate to every other, which fact being so
the culture entire, root, tip, is there
to be drawn from a lyric or webpage
properly understood, to outgrow
like a mouth on the Angel's hand,
buying time, asking for more,
privacy a fallacy and deadlines for all.
We want efficiency, not understanding.
That we're the sum of natural processes, fine,
are both happening and object but wholly neither,
a brand name to be pronounced
by any mouth on earth, made out by any ear.

II.

Begin Anywhere

Like a bank note in the open
I had everyone's attention

and I gasped like a pressurised plastic bottle
when upright it regains its shape.

I came to in the middle of things,
passed and passing, yes, to come,

a neighbourhood improvised like an argument,
a home subordinate to my parents' emotions,

and in those darker moments
I dreamt of transfusion,

an exchange of bloods, black 'n' blue,

and while the flesh of those around me
drooped and fell away,

I retained my youth
in the posthumous style of teeth.

Pop

Neglected billboard, and within the strata
of bleached ads, evaporated to an outline,
is a cartoon animal I recognise, the monkey
in shorts who brings a spoon, bowl and fresh
cow's milk to the jungle, voiced for a decade
by a woman impersonating a boy, ghost ad
waiting for the arrival of childhood.

Resonator Between Rains

Shattered agapanthus,
the injured heads of buddleia,
multi-pack rings and charlock,
a grease-proofed carboard box
with bone, and the last thing to darken
is fresh ballast on the track,
several shades off,
cued up for a later scene.

How many times the lights must've changed
since I made the decision to seduce him,
my dreams of him
were pure notation,
the repertoire of what happens
in every realised life.

Come Christmas
I gaze into the fir with my man
and find office space there.
I smile and agree
that the work-life balance should ease.

I say it's human to want to touch
a weeping co-worker when alone,
in an ascending lift, for example,
or at the sinks in the bathroom.

Money-Light-Money

Late nineties, BBC2, and the programming highlight
was *Moviedrome*, a showcase of reliably cult film
with the great Mark Cousins introducing (Cox gone
by the time I tuned in). Back from the pub, volume
down in case Mum was trying to sleep, already farther
than she knew from her offspring and own living room,
family snaps bathed in body horror, effects in the lens,
the shelving shadow-played by a notorious scene
in which the actors *allegedly* (they didn't), or plots
so stubborn they were almost heroic, each chosen
as a flick at the failsafe, loaned, already known.
For eyes wanting to adjust blockbusters we loved
gave out like mechanism, fit for purpose and lean
but to the newly adult mind as Power Point to dream.

The Interview

At this height, there's more time, more daylight,
a wind newly risen and fierce, and a lease
to the centre of the earth. Tabletop city
in geometric shadow. Construction sunset.

My blood-red host is gleeful on the phone,
the art being alone while anything but,
of having cake, being a voice in two places.
Few things are as superior as elsewhere.

Expert at not scaring the horses, he's loath
to give offence, a subtle investor for decades now
in the stubborn problem of Artificial Intelligence,
the longest distance between two points.

He quotes himself. Real wealth is metaphorical.
I go to make a note but power, he says,
mouth full, is knowing what to ignore.

The Amphibian

A featureless expanse, a flat beach
long enough and empty enough
for an almost painful brightness,

the one-way of any seaside, the series
of countless discreet journeys
into lesser form, jettisoned tyre, driftwood,
fishing wire, the glint of reducible crystal

and interrogated by that light and air,
somehow shameless in the churned water,
in the queasy truce following a storm,
a humanoid figure in superior metal

from a timeline of unknown origin,
one we'll reverse engineer,
distance the idea
that the past is a single direction.

The Resort

I walked an uninterrupted hallway,
glassless rooms recurrent in sunlight,
settled dust, scraps, one upright bottle,
five road tyres distanced like chairs.

The dermatological concrete dropped
in five broad steps to the sand, to
a barefoot wetness that was daylong shadow.
I took in the abandoned resort by backing up.
Unpainted. Halved. Amphitheatrical.

On the sand was an upturned boat,
a burnt-out circle, and the nearest lintel
sooted like a wearying eyelid.
There were names and instructions
on the seaboard wall.

The Star in the Branches

1.

As if every point on earth
ended in apex red,
cranes at distance and height
sing down the many miles
like our each communion with the moon.

2.

Sanity is distance from reality,
too far and you're anyone's,
too close and you're alone
like a saint in a coracle
glued to the build and drop of mercy.

3.

Landfall, and with it, omen after omen,
a gull pulls a thread from an undead pigeon,
a restaurant bin wheels itself away,
then waking on the hour, queasy,
the lone fish-scale of aftermath.

4.

What guarantee do I have of the journey?
I began and ended this way.
Did anything result, like a scar?

5.

Who of us can identify a leafless tree,
ochre in the fissures
and a star in the branches
like the incursive heavens themselves
will match any pace that we set?

III.

Kouros

He was looking at me, I know it, he was looking at me.
We both were looking at the same stone. We were looking
at each other through the stone.
— Odysseus Elytis, 'The Presence'
    (trans. Jeffrey Carson and Nikos Sarris)

I.

like a tree is
without choice
the kouros

there is either
extinction
or one tenable place

2.

wide path away
from cafes
whitewashed boles

path a consensus
of multi-faceted stones

and in jigsaw shadow
what we take in

is a raised hull
streaming with lizards

3.

our hire car is at rest
on hillside dust
and lines and lines of code

the stone head likewise pillowed

sun and moon in unblinking pursuit
wreathing stars

the kouros
awaiting upload

4.

meant perhaps
to mark a grave

the kouros a commission
one-off

or preempt
like a coffin

just as everyone
shouldering children
or holidaying

scratching ear, arm, belly button

infers the grave of someone

5.

under restless quercus
the kouros

called into time for what?

commemoration
renewal

dawn no bigger than a hand

the journey upward

through rain
like a star-field

through sun

6.

the toppled bin for village waste
emptied of adult things

is a playhouse
where wind accelerates

runs weightless pages of a phone book
a relic

numbers and codes
assigned to the living

7.

within earshot
of the quietly irrigated orchard

we hear and later see

a man
twist a stick
into a ring

armature
for eager children

picnic table
heaped with meadow flower, ox eye,
limoneum

and gasping
foliage

8.

in a poem by Elytis
a kouros

darkens
the centred Cyrillic

like sunstroke blackens
the aromatic earth

where a heavy head can be lain
an artificial man

mute and resisting of time

become background

9.

olive or quercus
broadcast

a unique
morphology

fork with cross-knots
scars and defects

avid
and slant
upward and downward

for earth
and for light

a hyphenated thirst

10.

the other end of the orchard
heaped and fire-damaged firewood

black branches
virtuosic with thorn

childhood threat
of snake or lizard

white ash, reptilian bark
a collapsed wall still useful

11.

a dry stone
with siblings

has dribbled away
to rubble

cushioned on silence
the largest
like a severed head

what may have been a groan
or a yawn

unwanted freedom
in a mouth

no longer correspondent to a lung

12.

the best phrases are worn stone
a pleasure to handle or make fit
anonymous, blackly humorous
subtle fragments of mass assent

13.

any olive is individual

picking through orchards
middle of the afternoon
I can only properly remember one

redirections in the bark
like slack on a lizard's neck

an outbreak on the bole
like a tumour

tiny fruit
two-tone leaves

in what little wind
made it past

mutant brothers and sisters

14.

in deepest America
other bank of a dried up river
a dust devil

short when feinted
tall, straightened

I thought it might glide down across the channel of rocks

but it stood in imitation

and from restless vortices
from granular rubbish and topsoil

a human sum

15.

a girl in sportswear
the owner's daughter

brings us fresh geranium
and an ashtray

unfolds on our behalf
the paper tablecloth

a map of the island

and refills our water
before we think to ask

16.

while we eat
or read of other things

we continue to watch
the kouros

pillowing ground more complex

sun stepping away
shadow drawn into each arid stalk

fragrant patches thrown
by the orchard

the fig relaxing

like someone
at evening

practicing scales

secretly accomplished

believing themselves alone

IV.

The Marine Freedom of Ceilings

The upturned restaurant overnight
and outsize bulbs like knots in a rope
take the depth of front of house,
when we ate here those bulbs
had a life in the street, the orphaned tree.

I'd call it your dream
but the word's too small
and what you called it yourself
I didn't catch, you don't quiz
when something's that painful to tell.

In that bedroom of yours
your doll-sized double appeared,
nearer to your face than mine was now.

It stood on the ceiling, head down,
clothes and hair neat, mouth
half-open, as if to speak - but instead set off,
room to room and house to house,
admissible as a ghost.

The foam in my coffee spoon shrank.

People eating, touching, watching TV,
ceilings blank and cracked as snow,
a weightless bulb on a wire,
lone as though prized, a head high flower,

and further on a chandelier,
the festoons more spectral flesh than glass
like a sea-trench evacuee, an emblem of limit.
It'd come far enough.

Some of the rooms were newly dark.
It had to feel its way back, picture frames,
switches, cords, top-of-wardrobe dust,
haul itself up through open doorways
back to the woman asleep at last.

Remote Things

I ate a well-travelled grape
from immaculate pantone fingernails.

I pictured the hotel entire, Bratislava,
corridor after corridor of rutted carpet

and muffled noise, of recessed chairs,
ashtrays in red Italian marble,

the decor
of a less innocent era

of therapeutic tobacco
and avian insignia.

Footfall

We knew jasmine, its reach
into public space,

and knew the clash
of a football against bellying mesh,

emptiness
by the dwindling carton

tracing a figure on paving stone,
the one which gulped

in its socket, loosened over time
by rain and the tread

of a thousand of us out,
a thousand of us back.

Three Mouths

1.

The better a stone
the more detail it holds,

a gasping statue
occupied by a god.

2.

The cartoonish mouth
of a fountain in Rome,

staunch eloquence,
spatter and brazen slime.

3.

I can't un-hear my own
cracked whisper, the time

my dry mouth
coughed your name.

Likeness

So raw a stone
is contradiction,

is glass and metal,
tarmac, black ice,

but no one thing enough,
each texture

deaf to its neighbours
and unseen

but drawn
to this non-surgical

edge, racked to this prow
of reunited

skin. Begin there,
reposition

the chisel
as it ticks

beneath what
is meant, what accident,

and cannot wound
but only touch

the wet mouth,
the pious unblinking eye.

A Berlin Evening

Other early lights on, higher or lower,
in the block the side of Yorckstrasse
I can see, a pendant passed beneath

by a man called to hidden rooms
or the brief timer on a landing,
an uplighter on full for a team meeting,

all of whom gesture like TV presenters -
that sense of total audience -
taking broadcast turns to speak, one

after the other bar one, a listener,
who rubs eyes to reveal, what?

Earthbound stars, unreachable
fires on a neighbouring mountain.

The View from Here

The watercolour sky
prophesied in childhood,
that inborn blue,

a pencil of yellow wood
to overwork
the scrap

of rationed paper
and learn

that effort alone
guarantees nothing,

stopping is a part,
submission a part,

new ways for the old pain.

2.

In all directions
infinite,

the night sky
never white,

as above a birth,
a mobile
of constellated trauma,

skin risen
under the sign
of allergen

and reactions
don't begin with us

if parents
are what we think with.

3.

A lit cigarette
through a piece of silk,

fresh recession,
kohl peephole

onto what's farthest down,
most stubborn,

green rose, blue rose,
white crow, black swan,

one-off breach for which
there's no lone word,

did I live it
into being,

or was I
given it?

Is it mine to lose
or gain?

Outside
childhood,

the trauma
of any hapless ancestor,

what is most beautiful
always

is the failure
to cohere.

Temple Meads

Intending to rise as prince of the lonely dabblers
in lipstick and electronics, I plucked a musty kerchief
to become famous with, would bring down into music
those indignities endured daily til they shrank,
a sea-change my acclaimed late albums would confirm.
I almost began…waterfront never meant to be lived in,
Bristol's welcoming curvature, promise of departure,
that fulcrum in particular, where you can toe the feeling
of being deserving, having earned uncontaminated time,
the inside of which is dream without waste, turning up
selfhood against westerly, the owner of knowledge
never looked for, achieved neutrality, a commute most
acutely felt after core hours on a Friday, push through,
tilt like the eye of an attendant gull, then bundling down
from derelict sorting office to high-numbered platform.

Underworld

Withheld rain
darkens like fruit,

curls white light
to a filament

about to pop from the heat.
That stubborn puddle

registers
our underworld

of exaggerated colour,
holds in trust

the glowing sheer
of a freshly risen high-rise

and a single
forgotten window.

V.

The Way Out is Through

This terrain of images again, deranged city
of youth, changed and nowhere a latch,
no survivor from which to spiral out, it

almost pushes back, the city won't cede
to a single brain, the one eight millionth,
less, of a sum never held as a whole,

Edwardian post box, Spanish plane packed with stone,
preliterate pub sign, the eyelets of a fence
detuned by rain, markings set down with the care

of a musical score, needing movement for fullest
expression, travel before the nuance will out,
then portioned electrified space for trespass

and the non-stop to Heathrow,
the supermarket carpark fills and empties
in the same or different ways, chained trolleys

and a stubborn outlier on the marled tarmac,
light industrial park, studios, recycling, a tower
and banner, 'Homes for Sale', a youngish man

smokes in the glass Juliet, a pop-up carwash,
brooding substation in brick and persuasive silence,
a brim-full skip, hardboard and skirting board,

a splintered front door. And the drugs
are many times stronger, the music more complex,
less embodied, a DJ will overcompensate,

send out plosive seizures of approval
between managerial tendings
of colourful laptop equipment,

an unwinnable argument, body and brain,
centred, distributed, we're old
but our music wanted to be whole

even if it'd always, knowing it, fail.
I text the group about him but if there are scraps
I don't already have they're withheld,

I don't push it and he hovers unlinked,
character without a script, actor on the wrong set
for whom there's no way back or forward or across,

creature of threshold, a great detective who steps
into a filmographic National Trust, the interior
of which awaits footfall in another space and time,

I clear my throat of 1920s phlegm, I resume,
who was the first to notice that childhood
was somehow further away than it should be,

who felt his parents' goodwill like an installation
he'd summon the wherewithal to dismantle,
who never knew the neighbours, the school

international, an undirected shout his soundtrack,
whose fear of regret told him memory was key,
that frustrating its birth by choice

was negligence not of past or present but future,
who saw beyond the consensus of sky
knowing deep space hides in plain sight,

drawn to accounts of limit experience
whether wartime, psychedelic or occult,
who read and read and read looking for an exit

from his precocious point of ingress,
who forbade our theoretical children
from ever owning Spare or Burroughs

after a breakthrough with their disruptive techniques,
who led the shuffling charge on behalf of a refuse truck
appeared like an apparition in the Saturday night street,

hi vis men, black bags by the neck, otherwise
ignored by the amber faces and mouths
turned to the high metal of the cage,

who once set off in search of a bus stop
where he could wait alone, smoke without being asked for one,
away from crowds and their dropped and rained-on food,

who saw a fox glide the camber of a suburban road
and at a boxed in bin do nothing less than rummage
like its arm was jointed like an ape's,

who didn't intervene when his broken down father
broke up his twenty first, merely shoegazed
as the guests left in a tussle of etiquette,

a genuine loner, of all of us the sole confirmed
now that parenthood and careers have pushed
the rest of us through that guise, somehow

odd to remember him in daylight,
the time I ignored the biro by the headboard
by making light of it, tunnels, spirals, lattice and cobweb,

the scribbled names of men and women, overwritten,
unreadable except (of course) yours and mine,
who would deafen himself with Aphex Twin,

drawn to the Elephant roundabout as if by tractor beam,
height of the CD single, any journey divisible
by the main track and its punctured remixes,

who shouted abuse at his Lynchian doppelgänger
standing undaunted unlit in the hallway,
bringing us out of adjoining rooms to see afresh

that turn of smallest light, a strategic mirror
(I emerged with someone not then my partner),
who walked with street lights responding directly

to being passed beneath, on/off/on, one painfully
early morning, him in just a hoodie, jeans and T shirt,
Converse hanging from some overhead wires

back near the club. Why did we leave him alone
when he needed us? He had something like a flat
in his parents' house and we envied him the privacy,

as we imagined it, he walked eight and a half miles,
they were fine but his feet were black, a detail
his parents found odd enough to ring round

and ask if there was a problem with drugs, this
before they'd seen his pupils at Sunday lunch,
"No problem", we said, thinking ourselves smart,

and who, bare-chested and ablaze on your parents' bed,
slept off *The Celestine Prophecy*
while the party surged, sweating things out

for the ascent to a high risen office when qualified,
who went linear like us, deferring instead
to clock time, spreadsheets and compound interest,

the wind-tunnel alley where he lunched, anonymous,
unreachable, who seems always to have been set apart,
marked in some way that defies sense and taste,

the obvious choice, either as one to be taken
or most actively seeking the limit he found
since all of it shrinks to a hippo toothbrush, 6+,

hilarious in our hands that hungover afternoon,
childhood flotsam, the charm of it contingent
on love for our friend as well as depictions of hippo,

not the monster but what lives in the marketplace,
the thought of him with it, his small, because very young, face.

Two Rivers Press has been publishing in and about Reading
since 1994. Founded by the artist Peter Hay (1951–2003),
the press continues to delight readers, local and further afield,
with its varied list of individually designed,
thought-provoking books.